SUPERBEUTS

MICHAEL JOSEPH PHILLIPS

ISBN 0-918342-19-8

First Printing December 1983

CAMBRIC PRESS
312 PARK STREET
HURON, OH 44839

INTRODUCTION

Michael Joseph Phillips, Ph. D., is, as his name and title suggest, a very respectable gentleman, scholar, and not very secretly—based on many publications—a poet. As a poet all the respectability fades and we see the writings of a voyeur wandering through the streets of a *Hustler* reality, outside, always outside, in praise of the hip, punk, whorish empress beauty in the coffee shop. The language is terse, bouncy, and will offend, yet there is more. For while Phillips appears to reduce women to their bodies for sale or simply their bodies, he also celebrates the pathetic in their lives, and more particularly in his own. So his poems are a tract of longing, at once adolescent and old, in which with skill and a certain madness, he has displayed his alienation from love, from women, from ordinary life. Where is there more humble praise than in the pitiful "cute empress Lulu" or in the confession to Samantha of his world?

Samantha

Beut go go wonder,
Finebuilt nightclub butterfly,
Michael's paramour !

This is Michael's world—where he is an exile to ordinary love. But in his acceptance of the paramour, the goddess, the doll, there is a curious pathos. It is the pathos of saying it as it is for now. Perhaps there will be another day of longing, and even fulfillment. For the moment he tells, in energetic gaudy language, the details of his present reality.

Willis Barnstone

ψαύην δ' οὐ δοκίμοιμ' ὀράνω δύσι πάχεσι

Sappho

Vivamus, mea Lesbia, atque amemus

Catullus

pacis Amor deus est, pacem veneramur amantes:
stant mihi cum domina proelia dura mea.

Propertius

How sweet it is!

Jackie Gleason

Dedicated to
Dick Higgins and Richard Kostelanetz

The author wishes to thank the editors, printers and publishers of the following newspapers, journals and books who first printed many of these works. Because of the frequency and quantity of my publications, I may here, as elsewhere, not have listed all my appearances in print—unintentionally.

ALL POETS AND WRITERS
ALTERNATIVE
BENTON COURIER
CAMBRIC POETRY PROJECT
COURIER
CRAFTSEED
INTERNATIONAL POETRY
NEW WAVE
OUTCH
THE POETRY
TRULY FINE
WRITERS ON WRITING

October 31, 1983

CONTENTS

Introduction	3
Alice	13
Angel	13
Angela Dorian	13
"Aradian dream"	14
Around	14
At 19	14
Audrey Hepburn	15
Audrey Hepburn	15
Barbara Carrera	15
Beut	16
Black Girl & Michael	16
Blonde	16
By A Rose	17
Candy	17
Candy VII	17
Cherry	18
Chicago Regionlike	18
Cindy	18
Club Doll	19
Crystal Gayle	19
Crystal Gayle	19
"Cultured madonna"	20
Cynthia	20
Date	20
Desire	21
Dish	21
Dolly Parton	21
Donna	22
Ellen	22
Empress	22
Erotic Concrete Waka	23
15 Yr Old	23
Fine	24
From Ohio	24
Futuristic	24
Greek Doll	25
Helen	25

"Hip Chicago beut," 25
Imagined 26
Imagined 26
In the Grocery 26
"Indy culture doll," 27
Jennifer 27
Jennifer 27
Judy 28
Karen 28
Kathy 28
Kathy 29
Lee 29
Libby 29
Manhattan Broad 30
"Manhattan pop queen," 30
Marsha 30
Mary 31
Model 31
Movie Lecturer 31
"neat Ivy League chick," 32
N.Y.C. Flower Girl 32
Newton-John 33
1955 33
No Girl Friend or Wife at 45 34
"North Beach art goddess," 34
Orient Express 35
Pam 35
Pamela 36
Patty 36
Peggy 37
Phenom 37
Prom Lady 38
Punk Rocker 38
Roberta 39
Rolling Queen 39
Samantha 40

Samantha 40
Samantha 41
Samantha 41
Samantha 42
Samantha 42
Samantha 43
Samantha 43
Samantha 44
Samantha 44
Samantha 45
Satori 45
Scherezade Reseen 46
Seen 46
Seen 47
Seen 47
Seen 48
Seen At I.U. 48
Seen 8/14/82 at Caveat
Emptor Around the
Card Section 49
Seen 11/20/82 49
Seen XIV 50
17 Yr. Old Girl 50
Sharon 51
Star 51
Susan 52
Suzanne Pleshette 52
Sworn To 53
Talked To Gal 53
Tammy 54
Tammy 54
Tammy 55
"Thames Flower
Beauty" 55
"Top U.S.A. Doll" 56
20th Century Gal 56
Vision of Euterpe 57
Waitress 57
Thoughts on Contemporary
Poetry 59

SUPERBEUTS

ALICE

Goddess N.Y.C. doll,
36'' x 24'' x 34'' dynamite,
Supreme poetess !

ANGEL

Queen d' paradise,
40''x 32'' x 34'' space doll,
Paragon d' cloud VII !

ANGELA DORIAN

All time ''Playmate'' star,
Hammocked a la hot hit trips,
Tanned hip pop mod doll !

Aradian dream
U.S.A. Aradian dream
Aradian dream

AROUND

Hot, hip street empress,
Legended whorish Cookie nymph,
Kirkwood's top hot fuck !

AT 19

Coffee shop princess,
37'' x 22'' x 35'' Bohemian doll,
Artist's paragon !

AUDREY HEPBURN

Fantasy princess,
European lady-queen,
Lucerne Swiss wonder goddess !

AUDREY HEPBURN

Go cosmopolite,
Sweet swing soft-talk Swiss princess,
European doll !

BARBARA CARRERA

Hot big hit empress,
Model paragon d' L.A.,
Top faced queen tempt-bit,
South American swing-chic,
Sultry hip beauty !

BEUT

Rosed golden lace-ace,
Action-sucker d' Hammond's bistros,
Space age tit fucker !

BLACK GIRL & MICHAEL

Ebony & Ivory,
Ebony & Ivory, Ebony & Ivory,
Ebony & Ivory,

BLONDE

Deutschland hit wonder,
Reformed democratic doll,
Hit "bunny" sex queen !

BY A ROSE

Flower power doll,
Blonde hip-pop *inspiration,*
Lover dynama,
82's black silk lace ace,
Hot untopped angel !

CANDY

Silked hot hustle dance-doll,
Black G'd Dior'd Ph. D.,
A. Hepburn empress copy !

CANDY VII

G-frocked dance empress,
$100.00 Space Age FANTASY,
Top Shannon Go doll !

CHERRY

Hot hip hit empress,
Paragon d' Kirkwood beuts,
Top U.S.A. flash —

CHICAGO REGIONLIKE

Top faced hot hip chic,
5'7'' tanned '82 coed queen,
Hit wundrus luv-flame !

CINDY

Beut boppop talker !
Powderpuffed sweet U.S.A. doll !
Leggy 100th Str. gal !

CLUB DOLL

A+ pace setter,
G-clothed Godiva hot saint,
Move virgin d' 82 !

CRYSTAL GAYLE

Beut song-singer wonder,
Magnificent pop chanteuse,
Highfine enchantress !

CRYSTAL GAYLE

Ivory chanteuse,
Top pop doll d' 82,
Exquisite empress !

Cultured madonna,
Schön Ave Maria bebop fan,
Fantastic doll !

CYNTHIA

Go go jive hopper,
Indianapolis doll,
"Concrete" paragon !

DATE

Punkdillyishus,
Rebecca, Rebecca, Rebecca,
Punkdillyishus,

DESIRÉ

Beut black silked lace-ace,
Bebop Meridian G-swinger,
Indy baby doll !

DISH

U.N. top space queen,
Divina Comedia,
Bluegreenbrown clad doll !

DOLLY PARTON

Finelove V-chanteuse,
Tennessee pop art warbler,
Queen de la *Country* !

DONNA

Daily Grind empress,
Blue jeaned 80's poet's queen,
Hit classical beut !

ELLEN

Artistic empress !
Zoot, cute baby-doll crafter !
Paragon d' Fine Arts !

EMPRESS

Flower powered queen,
Hot hip hit op-pop-mod doll—
T R A N S F I G U R A T I O N !!!!!!!

EROTIC CONCRETE WAKA

Rub a dub dub !
3 girls in a tub !
Rub a dub dub !
3 girls in a tub mit Michael !
Rub a dub dub !

15 YEAR OLD

Venus bop walker,
34'' x 20'' x 32'' Goddess,
Universal paragon !

FINE

Indy contessa,
Ah, delicate butterfly,
Sweet, beut Samantha !

FROM OHIO

Flower power doll,
Hip "day angel" wondrous one,
Venus goddess-child !

FUTURISTIC

Swing-doll d' 2100 A.D. !
Vampirella-Pantha beutgood queen !
Hot pop-castle goddess !

GREEK DOLL

Sweet hop-talk Venus !
Vesuvian golded breast-pyramids !
Athenian pearled V-beut cluster !

HELEN

Cambridge aca-doll,
Brained Ph. D. socialist masseuse,
Hit trip d' 82 !

Hip Chicago beut,
Top State Street paragon,
Ace luminescent !

IMAGINED

Flower power doll,
Inter-galactic   space ace,
Black haired hot goddess !

IMAGINED

Powderpuffed rockette,
Black silk G'd immaculate Manhattanite,
Punk rock hip paragon !

IN THE GROCERY

Cute blonde bebop beut,
35" x 22" x 34" teen age dynamite,
Built 15 yr old pop phenom !

Indy culture doll,
Sweetheart of op pop mod poets,
Commendable queen !

JENNIFER

Berlin WuNdeR-gal,
Voluptuous BATIK-clad doll—
Ah, BLACK platinum gems !

JENNIFER

Delux-volup top good gal,
Terre Haute "street cello" performer,
U.S.A. sensitive one !

JUDY

Indy bop-talk hot pop empress,
Sweet U.S.A. sense-gal d' Meridian St.,
Paragon d' love's virtues !

KAREN

Stewardess sex queen,
Photo hot set strip model,
Manhattan punk doll !

KATHY

Hot boogie sweet-meat !
Flower power paragon !
Bloomington express !

KATHY

Top go move maker,
Beut legged Tennessee gal,
Shannon's paragon !

LEE

Soft Aegean dream,
Hot Peloponnesian doll,
Sapphic wonder gal !

LIBBY

Go café empress,
Hot hipped coffee gal paragon,
Waitress swing divine !

MANHATTAN BROAD

"Tootsie Wootsie" doll,
43rd Street Curleycue Empress,
Tinsel set goddess !

Manhattan pop queen,
21 & beut punk-keen intellectual,
N.Y.U. playmate—

MARSHA

Beut car wash work queen,
Blonde, hot action seductress,
Hit laborer d' 82 !

MARY

Matchless feminist,
Therapeutic yea sayer,
Healer d' top hurts !

MODEL

Top Dior Goddess,
37'' x 25'' x 34'' Paris star-queen,
82's tailored silk-doll !

MOVIE LECTURER

Hot aca-starlet,
I.U.'s most glamrus op-prof,
Ah, yur gal film-talk !

Neat Ivy League chick,
Clean coed d' 82 stuff,
America's top trip !

N.Y.C. flower girl,
Paragon d' 57th & 5th Ave.,
Manhattan beauty !

NEWTON-JOHN

Ah, Olivia—
Boogie woogie punk sweetheart !
Ah, Olivia—

1955

Miami go girl,
Ah, empire-move hot empress,
Beut-dance pop phenom !

NO GIRL FRIEND OR WIFE AT 45

Blackness—
A go go dancer—
Some light !

North Beach art goddess,
Hip queen d'1982 beats,
Sultry black-haired empress !

ORIENT EXPRESS

Draw-shorted China doll,
Leggy August fantaztress,
Peking punk empress!

PAM

20th eon waitress doll,
Minnesota Art-Ed Venus Goddess,
Vermeer pop model !

PAMELA

Masai-like empress,
Ah, yur beaded Afro G-string,
"Dynasty" pinup !

PATTY

Attractive trickster,
Hot flower power empress,
Smooth female love boat !

PEGGY

Coffee shop hot doll,
Boogie Woogie hip empress,
1982's gal paragon !

PHENOM

Stacked tan star-fire,
Dark Hammondlike top goddess,
Love algebra hot-doll !

PROM LADY

Cute empress Lulu,
Top dance queen d' N.Y. hops,
Sultry enchantress !

PUNK ROCKER

Black & blue clad goddess,
37" x 23" x 35" go empress,
Downtown's paragon !

ROBERTA

North Central Go-child,
M.F.A. top U.S.A. empress,
Grad School dynamite !

ROLLING QUEEN

Beut U.S. skatc doll –
Dior roller disco cloth—
Wind, speed & wheels—

SAMANTHA

Beut go go empress,
Shannon's gorgeous paragon,
83's top doll !

SAMANTHA

Beut go go empress,
Sweetest silked loveboat d' 83,
All time dance goddess !

SAMANTHA

Beut go go wonder,
Finebuilt nightclub butterfly,
Michael's paramour !

SAMANTHA

Club-frocked genius,
Beut-breasted go world all star,
Top sex-hopper d' 82 !

SAMANTHA

Go-fine V empress,
Beut-built Indy butterfly,
Sky high move maker !

SAMANTHA

Go gal paragon,
Evansville hit hot dancer,
Arabian dream,
Magnificent V swinger,
True all world rockette !

SAMANTHA

Go go courtesan,
High paradisical empress,
Wonder demimonde !

SAMANTHA

Go go goddess-beut,
Paramour 'n silvered diamond,
Sweet south Indy doll !

SAMANTHA

Hot go go all star,
Built "stairway to paradise,"
Honky tonk angel !

SAMANTHA

Love set paragon,
Venus-genius empress,
All time go all star !

SAMANTHA

Wundrous lush lipped beut,
"Dish"-wish go hot goofy butterfly,
Great "cookie" baby-doll !

SATORI

Hot Tokyo punk gal,
007 Spa Goddess,
Sheik Oriental !

SCHEREZADE RESEEN

Hot Baghdad paragon,
Arabian harem sex goddess,
Hot top lace trickster !

SEEN

Dow Jones biz-empess,
Hot capitalistic nymphette,
43'' busted knockout !

SEEN

Hot tooty fruit doll,
Empress-genius d’ 82’s I.U.,
Goddessa VII !

SEEN

Slcck U.S.A. doll !
A. Hepburn Temple Goddess !
195 I.Q. ’d sugar !

SEEN

Wundrus go bod-doll,
Fantasy empress d' 82,
Queen cum paragon !

SEEN AT I.U.

Funky-wunk op sweetheart,
Hot black mystic queen-goddess,
African star-doll !

SEEN 8/14/82 AT CAVEAT EMPTOR AROUND THE CARD SECTION

Sultry, tan hip beauty,
Bloomington Scherezade,
1,001 night wonder !

SEEN 11/20/82

Blonde Eurasian beut,
Daily Grind Coffee House queen,
All time star empress !

SEEN XIV

Galaxy doll 7,
Cutetantallthin built XXX rated empress,
Real life hot street fuck !

17 YR. OLD GIRL

Beut 37'' x 22'' x 34'' !
New flower power pop talk !
Gal-silk satori !

SHARON

Analyst top goddess,
Psychiatric super pop doll,
Warm Oxford sweets queen !

STAR

Sault Ste. Marie queen,
Black & blue clad punk goddess,
Canadian dish—

SUSAN

Je vous aime beaucoup
"Miss right" in blue-gold Dior cloth,
Je vous aime beaucoup !

SUZANNE PLESHETTE

Beautiful lady,
Sweet dream du 70's bright lights,
N.Y.C. sophisticate !

SWORN TO

Go hot hipped flash queen,
Excellent Vegas show empress,
Butterfly supreme!

TALKED TO GAL

Space age leg lace ace,
Comparative Lit. Major
Space age leg lace ace—

TAMMY

Georgia bubble bath queen,
Atlanta hot bistro stunner,
Rhythmic bop goddess !

TAMMY

Lush hipped Wunderdoll,
Voluptuous slick Rubenesque sugar,
Moralbeut fine-lined empress !

TAMMY

U.S.A. rock doll,
Virtued computer major,
Disciplined coed !

Thames flower beauty,
Mini min skirted Windsor ace,
Top legged pop queen !

Top U.S.A. doll,
Hot Manhattan pop style queen,
Washington Square blonde !

20TH CENTURY GAL

Pop poem phenom—
Mod existential Christ doll—
Top surreal pure one—

VISION OF EUTERPE

Beut torsoed Greek goddess,
Black haired Ionic wonder woman,
Ah, shimmer empress !

WAITRESS

Bermuded West Coast gal,
San F. California dream,
Grad extraordinaire !

THOUGHTS ON CONTEMPORARY POETRY

A recent poll has shown that the *Nation,* the *New Yorker,* and *Poetry Chicago* are the country's most respected poetry periodicals. I assume the poll was taken among professors, etc. who have studied poetry in our universities. I have known quite a few great poets of the age, and the opinion of most of them of the work published in these journals is negative.

Competent concrete artists, such as Emmett Williams or Mary Ellen Solt, could make mincemeat of most if not all of the verse published in these magazines. Capable haiku artists, such as Elizabeth Searle Lamb or Lee Richmond can write circles around the poets appearing in them. Good regular poets such as David Wade, Garcia J. Villa, or myself barf at the poor titles and the lousy first lines, and discontinue reading after an initial perusal of this flimsy verse.

Has any poet (except Longfellow) ever lasted who was affiliated with a university? I welcome my status as an independent, and since I don't have to keep my shoes shined for the tenured exploiters, fogies and conveyors of falsehoods about contemporary poetry, I can read with my eyes open. I learn primarily from the classics and do not have to suffer the horrendous academic routine that is so prone to produce mediocre work among writers.

About what is published by the respectable publishing houses and university presses, I have this to say: it is fatal historically, and I can hardly believe how bad poetry is getting to be. Just because in the old days a house published Eliot, cummings, or Pound doesn't have anything to do with what they publish now, nor is it true that just because a press is associated with an educational institution, their poets are writing the best poetry. This vague association of presitigious publishing houses and university presses with mystical mysterious value is appalling.

I studied new criticism, and one of the most appealing calls was to look at the poem itself. But I saw that most new critics were puritanical despite their philosophical and moral depth. I.A. Richards probably has done more unintentionally to hurt taste than anyone else. Whoever reads Richards should balance this with Pound's *ABC of Reading* and *Letters.* Thematic inadequacy, formal clumsiness, and the absence of Homeric, beautiful, powerful vocabulary are the big faults now.

I suggest that what is needed is new thinking and textbooks about what great poetry is; comparative lyric study from a world point of view; and discussions as to what a great poem is by comparing poems and determining just what it is that separates Sakespeare's sonnets, Catullus, Sappho, Tzu Yeh, *et alii*, from all the rest. Perhaps our poets should have a try at this greater tradition instead of writing like everyone else.

Maybe I am just a shallow or hippy punk rock poet. But if some of my poems have inspired people to love and sex, I will consider it not to have been in vain. Satisfactory love and sex are the closest things to paradise this life has to offer. In view of a potentially disastrous decline in population and family life in this country, I can't help but assert that a poet should help his readers to LOVE.

Michael Joseph Phillips
& Richard N. Hayton